TOWNLIFE

L. M. CULLEN

with the collaboration of
George Morrison.

GILL AND MACMILLAN

First published in 1973

Gill and Macmillan Limited
2 Belvedere Place
Dublin 1
and internationally through
association with the
Macmillan Publishers Group

Cover design by Cor Klaasen

Insights into Irish History
General Editor: L. M. Cullen, Ph.D.

Other titles in the series
Merchants, Ships and Trade, 1660-1830 L. M. Cullen
Domestic Industry in Ireland W. H. Crawford
Landlord and Tenant in Nineteenth-Century Ireland James Donnelly
The Development of Technology in Ireland W. A. McCutcheon

309.14i6
(2)

Printed and bound in the Republic of Ireland
by Lithographic Universal Ltd.

Contents

Introduction

Insights into Irish History is a series in which it is intended to look at a number of topics chosen because they have a central significance or importance in Irish economic and social history.

The intention is not to analyse the topic or to present a mass of relevant detail. The early stages of learning or reading history rely heavily on generalisation, and introductory accounts or textbooks necessarily present a simplified picture in which abstraction tends to overlay the historical character of the period or subject. The purpose of the series is to avoid generalisation or abstract description, and to portray the topics simply in images drawn from contemporary documentary evidence and visual material. These are not selected for the purpose of providing students with experience of handling evidence; they are chosen simply because they provide a glimpse — descriptive or visual — of life as contemporaries saw it and in the terms in which they chose to depict it. Abstraction or generalisation is thereby avoided, and the descriptive and visual material — chosen for its relevance — should help the reader or student to see the essential features of social or economic life without the interposition of a pattern of abstraction or interpretation.

Each book in the series is complete in itself. But it is not intended to be read in isolation. The books are intended either for the general reader who has already some general knowledge of the historical framework or for teachers who wish to supplement the basic textbook in the schoolroom by the introduction of topics which will give the student a more down-to-earth appreciation of the economic and social background. In the case of schools, the books are intended primarily for twelve to fifteen year olds, but may also be useful in introducing older students to the social and economic background.

L. M. Cullen
Trinity College, Dublin.

3

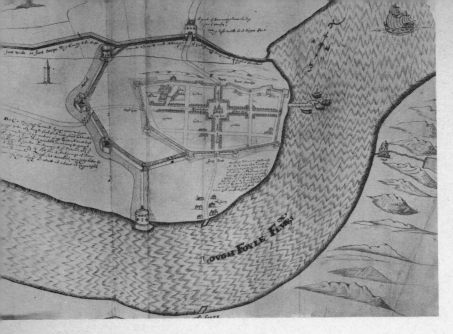

The walls and town of Waterford at the end of the fourteenth century. This is the earliest depiction of an Irish town.

Map of Londonderry, early seventeenth-century. The regular street-pattern, easily identified, contrasts with the less orderly street plan of medieval towns. Compare the character of Derry with that of Kilmallock.

Map of the walled town of Kilmallock 1600. Kilmallock is a good example of an Irish walled town. Note the mills — all six — on the river outside the town. Mills — watermills or windmills — were essential to grind the grain which country people brought to market and which was the staple of the townspeople's diet.

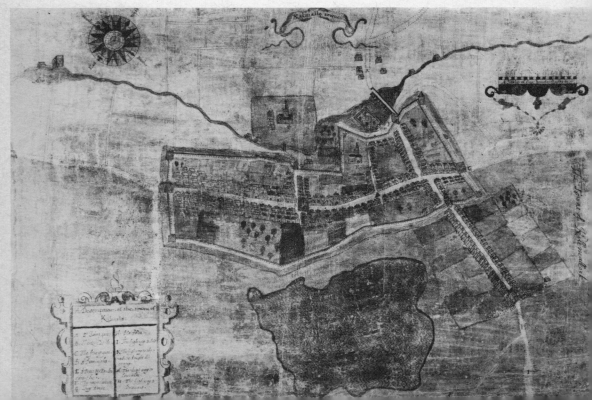

Town Walls

In medieval times every town of consequence was surrounded by
walls. Medieval life was insecure; townsmen also feared the
depredations of feudal magnates or of their lawless followers. The
central government was on the side of the townsmen, but it was
ineffectual, relying on the very magnates themselves for en-
forcement of its laws. Faced with this situation, townsmen erected
and in towns like Cork, Waterford and Dublin they were
from the line of wall, to make defence more effective. Walls still
served a purpose in the seventeenth century. New planned towns
like those of the Ulster Plantation were protected by walls. In many
older towns of strategic importance, the walls were even rebuilt to
make them more impregnable than ever before. The walls had
originally been erected at the citizens' expense for purely local
defence. But in the great struggles of the seventeenth century
when the fate of the whole kingdom was at stake, the fortifications
of major towns were rebuilt at royal expense.

Town walls rising massively above the surrounding green fields
were therefore still a feature of the seventeenth century. But as the
extension of royal authority had put an end to sporadic local
violence, the citizens became increasingly reluctant to undertake
the expense of maintaining the walls, and, outside the towns of
strategic importance where royal funds extended the fortifications,
the walls were already bearing signs of growing neglect. After
1691, with little prospect of any nation-wide challenge to royal
supremacy, the function of the walls seemed to have disappeared,
and in towns like Cork, Waterford and Dublin they were
quickly demolished to make way for expansion of the town.
Elsewhere only inertia saved the walls. In towns where there was
little urban growth, there was little pressure to demolish the walls.
Where there was no expansion, space was not at a premium, and
builders were too few and too inactive to need raiding the walls for
material. Youghal, for instance, had an impressive circuit of wall in

5

The gun emplacement on the wall of Galway and the four cellars beneath, are clearly indicated on this sketch, made over thirty years before the previous one. The gun emplacement itself was constructed in the early seventeenth century, and is not part of the medieval wall.

The walls of Drogheda as seen in 1698 1699 from the west by Francis Place. The road in the foreground leads up to gate and tower. The sketch conveys a good impression of the appearance of a walled town from the exterior, in particular the abrupt transition, before towns began to spread, from the countryside to the massive masonry of the walls.

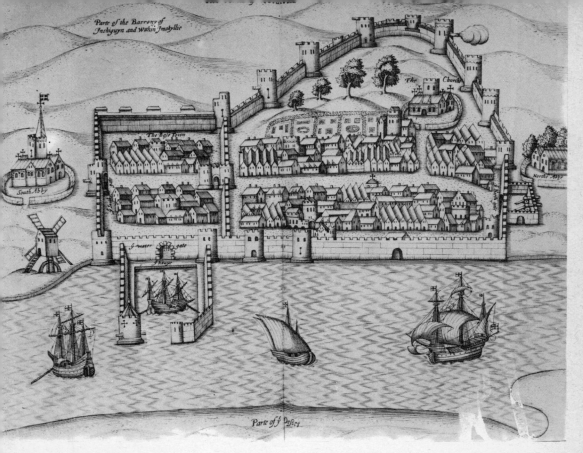

The walled town of Youghal in 1633.

Youghal over a century later, in 1750.
Note the limited expansion of the town,
and the good state of preservation of the
walls.

1633; the town still retained much of the circuit more than a century later. In general the more active the town, the quicker the walls were breached and pulled down. Traces of the walls in Cork and Dublin are few today because rapid expansion in the eighteenth century was responsible for their speedy demolition. Towns like Athenry and Kilmallock, on the other hand, retain large stretches of their walls because they have never prospered in recent centuries. In busier towns, little survives beyond the isolated gate or stretch of wall. In many instances an association survives only in a street name.

The only exceptions to the dismantlement of the walls of major towns were, apart from Derry, the ports of Limerick and Galway.

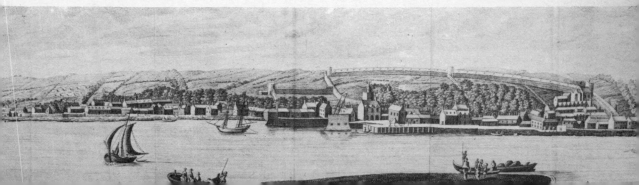

The possibility of Jacobite invaders making a successful link-up with the Catholics, regarded as disloyal, in the hinterland of these two towns, seemed the only threat to the security of the kingdom. An effort was made — unsuccessfully — to limit the residence of Catholics in these two towns deemed to be the bastions of royal power in the west of the island. These were the only towns in which a serious effort was made in the eighteenth century to maintain the walls in defensive repair. As late as 1740 in Limerick, funds were expended on repairs, and gates were renewed in Galway in 1747 and 1748. The gates were closed at night, sentinels mounted the walls, and in Galway during the Jacobite scare in 1745 the gates, normally open until ten o'clock at night, were closed at four in the afternoon. Maintenance was, however, already an uphill task. There were breaches through the walls in Galway into private yards in the 1730s; efforts were made to seal them, although without great success. After 1746, with the rout of the Pretender in Scotland, fear of invasion receded and maintenance was totally neglected.

The walls of Derry in the early nineteenth century. The French visitor, De La Tocnaye, had noted a few years previously that 'the ancient ramparts are not demolished but form at present an agreeable walk'. He thought that the town would be made more healthy by levelling them, thus 'affording a supply of fresh air'. He also suggests the reasons for the walls surviving intact: 'the inhabitants consider them as a glorious monument which reminds them of the siege this city held against King James'.

8

LIMERICK

The fortifications of this place have been useless many years;
houses are built on and close to the walls in many places; part of
the ramparts are taken down, so that it can no longer be deemed
a place of defence . . . The (Ordnance) Board are of opinion, that
to rebuild the fortifications at this place seems unnecessary, and
therefore have made no estimate thereof.

GALWAY

The fortifications of this place, like those of Limerick, are in
many places in ruins, and have not had any repairs to them for a
great number of years. The sum it would take to make this place
defensible and supply it with ordnance and ammunition, would
be very great.

Only the slow growth of Galway halted the physical removal of
the walls. By the end of the century private houses had in many
cases encroached on the walls, and passage on them was no
longer feasible.

There are no gates at this end, but a great rampart with bastions
still stands around the town. These walls could provide an
agreeable promenade if each of the neighbouring houses had
not appropriated part of them. The quay is the popular
promenade. The walls rise perpendicularly and are very high
and very thick. They serve no purpose now except for ball
games. Some cannon without gun-carriages are still upon them.

Town Growth

In the middle of the seventeenth century towns within their walls
were small. Suburbs outside the walls were small as well. Dublin
was the only major exception with a substantial district already in
the earl of Meath's Liberties. Outside most walled towns, however,
the suburbs were modest, amounting to a large extent to a 'cabin
district' — in contrast to the more solid and elegant buildings of the
walled town — on the main approach road. But urban growth,
consequent on the progress of trade in the late seventeenth and
early eighteenth centuries, was to result in the creation of entire
new districts. In Dublin, for instance, the building of a second
bridge across the Liffey in 1678 was responsible for directing the
main expansion of the city to a new axis along the freshly-laid out
thoroughfare named like the bridge after the Lord Lieutenant of the
time, Arthur Capel, earl of Essex.

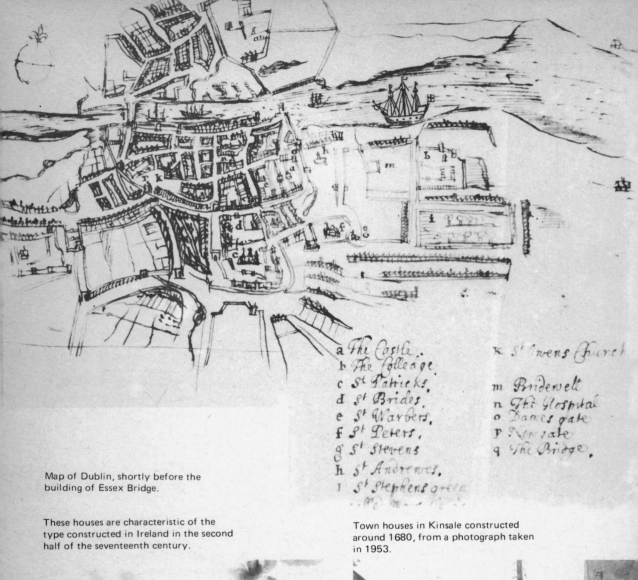

a	The Castle.	k	St Owens Church
b	The Colledge.		
c	St Patricks.	m	Bridewell
d	St Brides.	n	The Hospital
e	St Warbers.	o	Dames gate
f	St Peters.	p	New gate
g	St Stevens	q	The Bridge.
h	St Andrewes.		
I	St Stephens green		

Map of Dublin, shortly before the
building of Essex Bridge.

These houses are characteristic of the
type constructed in Ireland in the second
half of the seventeenth century.

Town houses in Kinsale constructed
around 1680, from a photograph taken
in 1953.

ENNIS
Its South East Prospect

Ennis as seen by the traveller Dingley in 1680. The buildings shown were erected in the 1650s and subsequently.

Expansion entailed house building. Houses in the second half of the century continued to be built in accordance with earlier patterns. One of the identifying characteristics of these houses was dormers, a feature imitated in many private houses and public buildings of the period. But active housebuilding also promoted the diffusion of new styles and new materials, which were rapidly adopted in the housebuilding of the late seventeenth and early eighteenth centuries.

Galway houses: fronts and courtyards. The sketch is from the 1650s; the houses themselves were erected a century or more earlier.

Stone houses Galway: nineteenth-century engraving of Galway houses.

Facade and courtyard of Rothe House, a
late sixteenth-century house in
Kilkenny.

Wooden house, Drogheda, erected 1570,
taken down 1824.

Last remaining wooden house in Dublin,
1834.

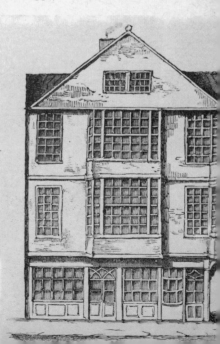

Houses depicted on both flanks of Baal's
bridge, from a map of Limerick, c. 1600.

Houses of stone had predominated in some towns like Galway, Limerick, and Kilkenny. These spacious stone houses, replacing medieval stone houses in the sixteenth century, were often built around a courtyard. In other towns, like Dublin, Drogheda, and Waterford, while stone houses were not unknown, timber remained a popular mode of building — the dominant house type of the mid-seventeenth century being large timbered houses constructed a century previously.

A revolution came with the use of brick popularised in Irish towns by Dutch immigrants in the second half of the century. It rapidly replaced timber and stone as the basic building material in housebuilding in Dublin even before 1680, and a decade or two later in the other port towns. The first brick houses were also built in a different style with the roof gable facing the street in imitation of Dutch houses. Brick could be imported cheaply to port towns; as fashion spread, bricks were baked from local clays. The new style and material were very evident in the Dublin Liberties which expanded from a small suburb to a populous and prosperous manufacturing district in the second half of the seventeenth century. They were also evident in the vigorous housebuilding characteristic of Cork, Limerick and Waterford after 1691.

The expansion of towns was inevitable. But the narrow streets, noisome atmosphere and congested thoroughfares of the central districts quickened the process of expansion by ensuring that the well-to-do would leave the old districts for the new ones that began to emerge as the century went on. These districts were characterised by wide streets, sometimes graceful residential squares, and larger and more elegant houses. Windows were larger, and the cramped dormer storey was replaced by an additional full storey. Wide Street Commissioners appointed in Dublin and Cork were responsible for superintending much of this work. Cork was no less striking than Dublin in the extent of the change. The medieval town, compact and small, was sited on one of many islands

Weavers' Square, Coombe, Dublin: early 'Dutch' houses.

Seventeenth-century 'Flemish' houses, still standing in 1913, Sweeney's Lane, Dublin.

Photograph of Nicholas Street front of Galwey's Castle, known as Ireton's House, Limerick, in or before 1894. The picture, taken shortly before its demolition, affords a dramatic glimpse of the fusion of two architectural styles. Originally a stone house, it was reconstructed in brick in or after 1691 and was reputed Limerick's first brick house.

Waterford from across the river in 1699.
The painting shows the quay wall,
similar to that of Galway or other towns.
Early in the eighteenth century it was
taken down, and houses erected on its
site.

Waterford in 1736, showing the houses
erected along the line of the old quay-
wall. Some are in the older fashion with
dormers. Most have their gables facing
the front in the new 'Dutch' or 'Flemish'
fashion.

Waterford in 1795. By this time the
house on the quays had been replaced or
rebuilt, mainly as a result of late
eighteenth-century activity. Many of the
structures are warehouses, in contrast to
Waterford in 1736 when the quay was
mostly fronted with residential
structures.

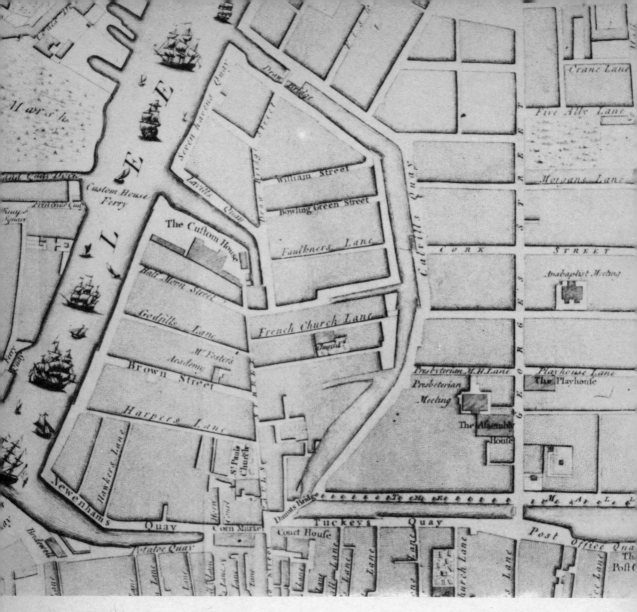

Names visible on the map:

Crane Lane · Five Alley Lane · Mergans Lane · Seven havens Quay · Draw Bridge · Marsh · Custom House Ferry · The Custom House · Lavitts Quay · William Street · Bowling Green Street · Faulkners Lane · Calvills Quay · CORK STREET · Anabaptist Meeting · Half Moon Street · Godfells Lane · French Church Lane · Mr Fosters Academy · Onguard · Knap's Square · Fitz Sior Quay · Brown Street · Harpers Lane · St Paul's Church · Presbeterian M.H. Lane · Presbeterian Meeting · The Assembly House · Playhouse Lane · The Playhouse · GEORGE'S STREET · Hawkers Lane · Newenhams Quay · Corn Market · Daunts Bridge · Court House · TUCKEYS QUAY · Post Office Quay · The Post O · Potatoe Quay · Bird well

separated by channels in the river Lee. Eighteenth-century Cork, with its picturesque but noisome river channels, presented a picture of congested traffic in narrow streets and in the approaches to the solitary bridge across the main or northern channel of the Lee. The gradual creation of new thoroughfares by the filling in of some of the channels at once eliminated much of the nuisance and solved the city's traffic problem, transferring it in the early nineteenth century from a cramped and dirty town, adversely commented on by travellers, into a spacious and even elegant city.

Cork in 1773, showing open river channels along the line of the modern St Patrick's Street and the South Mall. Another channel, foreshadows the modern Grand Parade.

16

During this eventful period many of the streets, previously engrossed by tide-filled canals, that exhibited, upon the retreat of every flow, disgusting accumulations of putrefying matter, were carefully vaulted over, and level and durable artificial causeways constructed. The adjacent swamps have been completely dried, the encroaching floods embanked, and many other improvements accomplished, suggested by considerations of health and beauty.

There exist in Cork two useful public bodies or boards — the Commissioners of Wide Streets, and the Harbour Commissioners. Their efforts to improve have not been limited to the exercise of the duties of their office separately and distinctly, but, in order to work out the best possible results, they have combined their strength and exertions, and have 'pulled together'. The consequences of this union have been most happy; the unsightly channel of the tide-deserted river is narrowed, and confined by a lofty quay-wall, faced with hewn stone, and extending for a length of one mile and a half, built at the joint expense of these two public boards. Two new stone bridges have lately been added to those that previously ministered to the convenience of the citizens. New gaols, new public roads, and promenades, a new Court House, Custom House, and handsome Commercial Buildings, are now to be annexed to the list of modern city embellishments, besides others of great utility, but of less attraction in their external decorations . . .

There are now many spacious and handsome avenues in this busy, bustling place; of these perhaps, none is more open, elegant, or graceful, than the South Mall. Let the equestrian statue of George the Second occupy the centre of the foreground, — let the river Lee, spanned by a handsome arch, of fair proportions, and of smooth wrought stone, come in to the right, — and, let the Mall itself be thrown into perspective, the distant wooded banks carrying the eye away beyond the extremity of the vista, and the arrangement will place the reader and spectator exactly in that position which the illustrator recommends as the most picturesque.

Three windmills on the northern fringe of Dublin. Windmills were frequently depicted in seventeenth and eighteenth century drawings of Irish towns. The surroundings of Dublin had many to supplement water power in grinding the city's food supply.

As towns grew their appearance changed. The growth of trade was responsible for the emergence of large warehouses in the late eighteenth century in or close to the quays of port towns. Many of the warehouses replaced residential houses constructed less than a century earlier. Industry, too, contributed powerfully to the changing face of the towns. Before 1700 industries were few and most of the industrial structures — water mills and windmills, — were usually sited in the suburbs. But increasingly after 1700, glasshouses, breweries, and even more noisomely, brickworks, lime kilns and salt works, vomited forth smoke and fumes in to central districts. A pall of smoke overhung the larger towns; in Dublin in 1772 steps were taken to ban some of the worst offenders — lime kilns and brick works.

New methods in the textile industries — the application of steam power to drive spinning machinery — resulted in a striking change in some towns in the early decades of the nineteenth

Glass house, Dublin, 1731, earliest depiction of a Dublin industrial structure.

Glass furnace, Dublin, 1749.

Flue or furnace of industrial works in central Dublin. The Custom House is in background.

A brewery. The brewer's cart was a common sight in the streets, and was frequently depicted in eighteenth-century prints.

19

Smoke from an industrial chimney in Cork, late eighteenth-century. This is the first artistic depiction of factory smoke in an illustration of an Irish town. Earlier artists had ignored it. As it became more prevalent, artists began to depict it, at first rather self-consciously and uncertainly like this artist.

Late eighteenth-century shop front.

Mulholland's mill, Belfast, c. 1840. Thackeray, visiting Belfast, noted in his **Irish Sketch-book**, 1843 that 'a fine night-exhibition in the town is that of the huge spinning-mills which surround it, and of which the thousand windows are lighted up at night-fall, and may be seen from almost all quarters of the city'

Preamble to an 1772 statute to prevent the baking of bricks in or near Dublin.

34
A. D.
1772.

The eleventh year of George III.

CHAP. VI.

An act to prevent the pernicious practice of burning bricks the city of Dublin, or the neighbourhood thereof.

Bricks not made or burned within two measured miles from the publick lamps,

WHEREAS large quantities of bricks are fre burned within the city of Dublin, and in the bourhood thereof, by means whereof the inhabitants said city are grievously annoyed, and the lives of many persons have been lost: for remedy thereof be it ena the King's most excellent Majesty, by and with t vice and consent of the lords spiritual and temporal an mons in this present Parliament assembled, and by the rity of the same, that from and after the tenth day of M thousand seven hundred and seventy one no person shal or cause to be made, burn, or cause to be burned, an within the distance of two measured miles from the lamps of the city of Dublin, on pain of forfeiting tho and ten shillings for every thousand bricks made or within the aforesaid limits.

or forfeit-
ed and 10s.
per 1000l.

Industrial housing in Belfast — Raphael Street, off Cromac Street, scheduled for demolition when this photograph was taken in 1912.

century. The machinery was housed in a great gaunt building not unlike the warehouses that already crowded the quays; adjoining the mill was the engine house with its tall chimney belching smoke into the atmosphere. One or two of these factories, added to the gaunt new warehouses, were a striking new dimension in many nineteenth-century towns in Ireland. In Belfast, in particular, a large number of these mills were erected, especially on the slopes to the

PIPEING hot, fmoaking hot, come and buye what I've got, hot Cakes hot: —One a-penny, two a-penny, diddle, diddle Dumpling Cakes

FRESH Butter, frefh Butter here— Here's the new Milk hot from the Cow—Maids, come for your Milk.— Here's fine rich Cream

BUYE my large new Potatoes;——
Here's green Pease, young Pease;——
Young Beans, large Winter Beans.

SHOES to mend, Shoes to mend——
Shoes or Boots to mend.——Have you
any Work for the Cobler to-Day
Madam?

BUYE the dry Turf; buye Turf;
buye the dry Turf.——Here's the dry
Bog-a-Wood.——Here's the Chips to light
the Fire; Maids!

WHO buys the Black-Pans? Who
buys the Black-Pans? Who buys?
——Here's the Earthen-Ware: Here's the
China, but where's the Money?

OLD Rug, old Rags; Have you any old Rags to sell?—Here's Ware for old Rags

Stalls were a common street sight.

west of the city, making it the only truly industrial town in Ireland. In the streets around the mills row upon row of two-storeyed brick houses were erected for the expanding labour force.

Another feature of the nineteenth century was the great increase in the number of shops. In the eighteenth century, apart from those selling luxuries, there were few shops. Most of the inhabitants made their modest purchases not only of food but even of clothes from street traders. Drapery and food shops became

Kilkenny Commercial House, c. 1840.

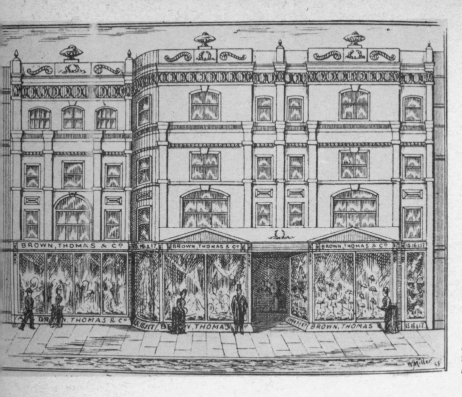

An engraving of a large shop front from Stratten's **Directory of Dublin, South and East of Ireland,** London 1892.

more common from the middle of the nineteenth century, and large department stores also made their appearance.

The continued growth of traffic was responsible for many changes in towns — the opening of new bridges to relieve congestion in cross-town traffic, the execution of major harbour works, and the erection of terminals for the railway network which began to emerge in the 1840s.

Continued growth of traffic was responsible for further street widening, such as the creation of Royal Avenue in the 1870s through the maze of narrow lanes and streets off High Street in the city of Belfast, and at about the same time in Dublin the cutting of Lord Edward Street through narrow streets of seventeenth or eighteenth-century housing beside the Castle.

The physical changes of the nineteenth century were very striking involving yet another stage in the move of the well-to-do further away than ever from the town centres, and within the central districts themselves the multiplication of warehouses and large shops, street widening, the erection of new or widening of existing bridges, and the execution of harbour works.

Opening of floating dock, Limerick,
1861.

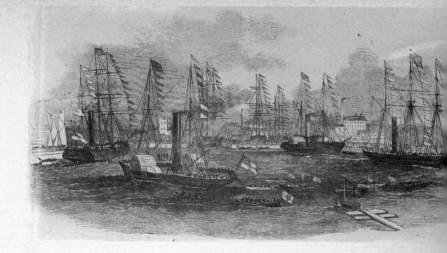

St Patrick's Bridge, Cork, 14 December,
1861.

Opening of new graving dock, Belfast,
1867.

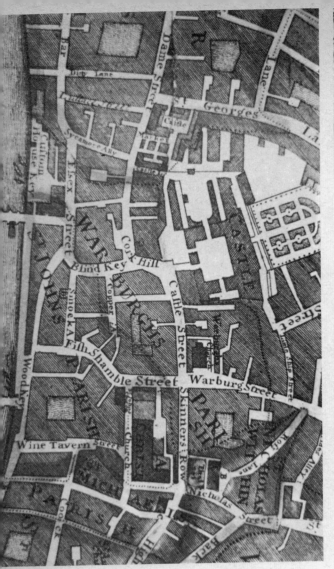

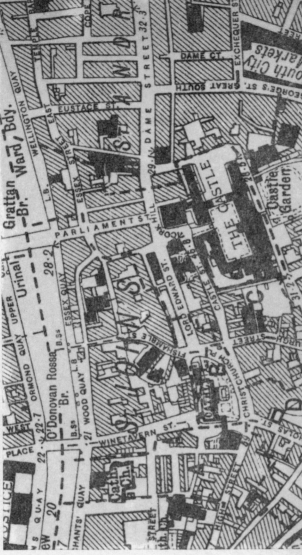

The making of new streets has been a continuing process in growing cities. The section on the left is from Brooking's map of Dublin, 1728, showing the narrow thoroughfares in the vicinity of the Castle. The section on the right is from a modern ordnance survey map for approximately the same area. Parliament Street from the Royal Exchange (now City Hall) to Essex Bridge, was executed in the 1760s. Lord Edward Street, built by clearing away old lanes and houses from the seventeenth and early eighteenth centuries, and providing a wide and direct thoroughfare from Dame Street to Christchurch Place, was undertaken more than a century later in the 1880s. Christchurch Place was produced in the process of clearance. Before this, it was hemmed in on all sides by buildings. Skinners' Row, a narrow street which had provided the main thoroughfare from the Castle to High Street, was cleared away entirely on the Christchurch Cathedral side. Viewed on the maps, the line of both Parliament Street and Lord Edward Street can be clearly seen to cut across older street patterns.

Housing

Housing more than any other single feature reveals living conditions. The poor often congregated in cabins on the commons or along the approach roads to towns. A striking contrast existed in pre-Famine Ireland between the ragged approaches and the neat, slated and prosperous houses at the centre.

The suburbs of the town of Kells contain the greatest misery which the Assistant Commissioners have ever seen in any country. To describe, therefore, the dozens of cabins there in which they found wretchedness and destitution under every form would be endless. Cabins of single rooms are there frequently occupied by a large family, with sometimes a widow or an old man lodging with them, or occupied altogether by several widows, or by one or more, and one or two old men, and all (pigs included) sleeping in the different corners of the room. The families are those of labourers, who generally get but very little employment; and the old men and widows subsist chiefly by begging, except those who are wholly or in part supported by their children, who give them all that they can spare of the wages they earn at service. The general state of their bedding and covering may, after what has been already stated, be better imagined than described. A number of these cabins are situated in little courts at the back of the main row of cabins which form the front of the street or road. These courts are seldom more than six or seven feet wide, and that space, which forms the only passage or entrance to the cabins, is usually blocked up with the heaps of manure made by the pigs, and with the rubbish and filth thrown out of the houses at the very doors. The following was the most deplorable case which the Assistant Commissioners met with: the cabin was only about eight feet by

Slated houses at the centre of Kells.

Street of thatched cabins on the approach to Kells, 1819.

A cabin outside Sligo, 1913.

Cabins outside Sligo, 1913.

six, and merely separated from the one adjoining by slight boards, or rather wide rails, with openings of one or two inches between many of them. There was neither chimney, hole in the roof, nor one in the wall, the door being the only aperture of any description for light, air, and smoke. The furniture consisted of one stool, an old kettle, a pot and a mug; a few handsful of straw, almost black with damp, rottenness, and filth, lay on the ground in one corner for a bed, and two or three pieces of old blanket formed the only covering. This cabin was inhabited by a man (a labourer in occasional employment), his wife, and two young children. They pay £1.5s. a year for rent, without even a yard to the cabin. The floor was exceedingly low and damp; the latter, indeed, it was sure to be, as it was situated in a narrow court, filled with dung-heaps half way up to the walls, and where it was almost impossible for sun or air to penetrate. The dreadful misery existing in the suburbs of Kells is attributed to the great number of poor, who are said to have come there, within the last 10 or 15 years especially, after being ejected from little farms or cabins in other parts of the country, being also attracted by the residence of landed proprietors in the vicinity, and by that of many genteel families in the town and neighbourhood, from whom they hoped to obtain employment and succour, as well as to partake, in time, of a small fund held by the corporation for the relief of the poor.

29

As an example we shall describe a house in Three Hatchet-lane, a populous part of the city: a sketch, with the dimensions, will serve to show the crowded state.

Description of slum accommodation in the city of Cork given in evidence before the Commissioners enquiring into the conditions of the poorer classes in Ireland, 1836.

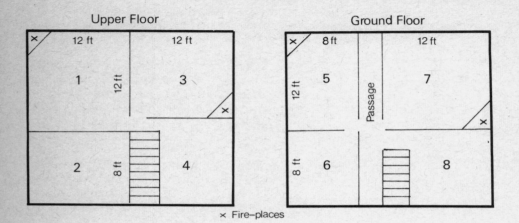

× Fire–places

Nos. 1 and 2 occupied by a shoemaker and his daughter: clean and decently furnished.

Number	Men	Women	Children	Total
3	1	1	4	6
4	1	1	1	3
5 and 6 . .	1	3	7	11
7	1	1	7	9
8	. .	1	4	5
Total . .	4	7	23	34

By leaving out Nos. 1 and 2, this gives a surface of about 16 square feet to each individual. The whole of these persons slept upon straw, very dirty and old, which was stowed in a corner during the day, or put into a box used as a seat; the only covering besides their day clothes were three rags of blankets amongst them all: pots to boil potatoes, and stools for seats, constituted the rest of their furniture. There was a little fire in two of the rooms only; it was a cold day in February. The men, excepting one who was sick, were out at work. Nearly the whole of the children were out, and stated to have gone begging: they go chiefly into the country, and return with potatoes given by the farmers. It may be observed, that of the women and children the greater number were healthy; some, however, on the contrary, appeared half-starved and sickly.

30

From the Rev. James Whitelaw's **Essay on the Population of Dublin** 1798.

In the ancient parts of this city, the streets are, with a few exceptions, generally narrow, the houses crowded together, and the reres, or back-yards, of very small extent. Of these streets, a few are the residence of the upper class of shop-keepers, and others engaged in trade; but a far greater proportion of them, with their numerous lanes and alleys, are occupied by working manufacturers, by petty shopkeepers, the labouring poor, and beggars, crowded together, to a degree distressing to humanity. A single apartment, in one of these truly wretched habitations, rates from one to two shillings per week; and, to lighten this rent, two, three, and even four families, become joint tenants. As I was usually out at very early hours on the survey, I have frequently surprised from ten to sixteen persons, of all ages and sexes, in a room, not fifteen feet square, stretched on a wad of filthy straw, swarming with vermin, and without any covering, save the wretched rags that constituted their wearing apparel. Under such circumstances, it is not extraordinary that I should have frequently found from thirty to fifty individuals in a house. An intelligent clergyman, of the church of Rome, assured me, that No. 6, Braithwaite-street, some years since, contained one hundred and eight souls. These, however, in 1797, were reduced to 97; and, at the period of this survey, to 56. From a careful survey, twice taken of Plunket-street, it appeared, that thirty-two contiguous houses contained 917 souls, which gives an average of 28.7 to a house; and the entire Liberty averages from about twelve to sixteen persons to each house. This is certainly a dense population: the best informed inhabitants, however, assert, that it was much greater a few years since, and to this opinion I willingly accede. I do not, however, affirm, that the houses, at present in existence, contained more inhabitants at any former period, though such probably was the fact; but I am confident that a great number of houses, that once teemed with population, are no longer to be found. These were situate in narrow back courts and lanes, off the principal streets, and their ichnography is distinctly expressed in Roque's four-sheet map of Dublin, which I generally found minutely exact. With this map in my hand, I searched for these courts: some had totally disappeared, and their entrances had been built up; the greater part, however, I found, but their houses were mostly in ruins, or converted into warehouses or work-shops, now perfectly useless; and the few that remained were in a state of rapid decline.

This crowded population, wherever it obtains, is almost universally accompanied by a very serious evil; a degree of filth and stench inconceivable, except by such as have visited those scenes of wretchedness. Into the back-yard of each house, frequently not ten feet deep, is flung, from the windows of each apartment, the ordure and other filth of its numerous inhabitants; from whence it is so seldom removed, that I have

31

seen it nearly on a level with the windows of the first floor; and the moisture that, after heavy rains, ouzes from this heap, having frequently no sewer to carry it off, runs into the street, by the entry leading to the staircase.

In the course of the survey, I frequently remonstrated with the inhabitants, and particularly when I found them unemployed and idle, on their not attempting to remove their dirt; but their universal answer was, 'It is not my business; if I remove it, who will pay me?' The landlord, who, in reason, should attend to this matter, seldom interfered. If he had an apartment in the house, the evil was, perhaps, somewhat less, though frequently he was the greatest brute in the stye. I found, however, that he was generally some money-grasping wretch, who lived in affluence, in, perhaps, a distant part of the city, and who made a trade of renting out such houses to the poor, with whose concerns he never interfered, except to collect his rents, generally weekly; in which, indeed, he betrayed no remissness whatever. Now, might not an act of the Legislature empower the magistrate, if he have not that power already, to make the landlord, who has generally an exorbitant profit rent from these miserable habitations, answerable, under a sufficient penalty, not only for their filth, but for their bad state of repair? This last circumstance is necessary to be attended to, as they very frequently admit every shower of rain, and sometimes, from their ruinous state, threaten destruction to the passenger. In July 1798, the entire side of a house, four stories high, in Schoolhouse-lane, fell from its foundation into an adjoining yard, where it destroyed an entire dairy of cows. I ascended the remaining ruin, through the usual approach of shattered stairs, stench and filth. The floors had all sunk on the side now un-supported, forming so many inclined planes; and I observed, with astonishment, that the inhabitants, above thirty in number, who had escaped destruction by the circumstance of the wall falling outwards, had not deserted their apartments. I was in-formed, that it had remained some months in this situation, and that the humane landlord claimed, and actually received for it, the usual rent.

22,324. Is it the fact that a large number of houses are owned by individual house farmers in Dublin? — A great number. A large number of houses in the older parts of the city are owned by families occupying good positions, some of them living in other countries. Jervis Street is owned by the representatives of Sir Christopher Jervis, who lived 200 years ago. Then Mr. Tankerville Chamberlayne, a well-known country gentleman, is the owner of a number of houses. These houses have been let at very small rents to house jobbers, who live by screwing the largest amount of rent they can out of the tenants. The disproportion between the rents which the actual owner of the

Evidence of Dr Charles A. Cameron, city medical officer of health before commission of enquiry into the housing of the working classes, 1885.

house gets and the rents which those house jobbers get out of the tenants is sometimes as one to three. I have scheduled a number of houses, showing the terrific rents which are got out of these old houses.

22,325. Would you mind giving us one or two instances? — Some of the houses are valued at 8£. and let at 70£. a year.

22,326. It has been stated by former witnesses that five house jobbers in Dublin owned 1,100 houses between them? — I think that is rather an over estimate; but there is a large number. I have known a case where a man had two houses that were in a perfectly insanitary state, and we got a magistrate's order to close them, and the man come to me and said 'It is a cruel thing closing these two houses.' I said 'they are quite unfit for human habitation.' 'Well,' said he, 'I will have to go into the poor-house if they are closed.' I said 'I cannot help that; you ought to get some other occupation.' He was a mere year-to-year man; he had not even a lease. He took two houses and he and his large family lived upon the produce of these two small tenement houses. I said 'that is not the way to make a living; you ought to have some other employment than screwing rackrents out of your unfortunate tenants.' The real owners of many of the houses get very little out of them, and as for the middlemen, whom I look upon as the curse of Dublin even the rents which they undertake to pay they sometimes do not pay. Then there is another great hardship, one of these middlemen takes a house on a 21 year lease; he pays 12£. a year rent, and he gets 10£. to 20£. from the tenants, and yet, if we want structural alterations done, we cannot even make that man pay for the expense of the structural alterations; and we make the head landlord pay, perhaps, 25£. or 30£. for putting in a water closet, all for the benefit of this middleman. We have no hold upon him at all. When we enforce structural improvements in houses I say that every one who has a beneficiary interest in the houses should be made to contribute to the expense of putting them in a proper state. I have known landlords have to pay so much money in improving their houses that for three or four years the rent altogether went in that direction; whereas in the meantime the middleman got his full rent.

23,250. Have you any notion at all of the average rents which are paid for rooms in those large houses in your neighbourhood? — Yes; the rents of the rooms would vary according to the position in the house. The people live of course from the kitchens to the garrets. The people in the front kitchen will pay 2s. per week; the people in the back kitchen will pay 1s. 6d. per week; in the front parlour they will pay 3s. 6d. per week; in the back parlour about the same; in the front drawing room about 3s. 6d.; and in the back drawing room about 3s. Then upstairs the rents will be 2s. 6d. and in the garrets above they will be

Evidence before the Commission on housing of the working classes, 1885, of rent levels in slum tenements.

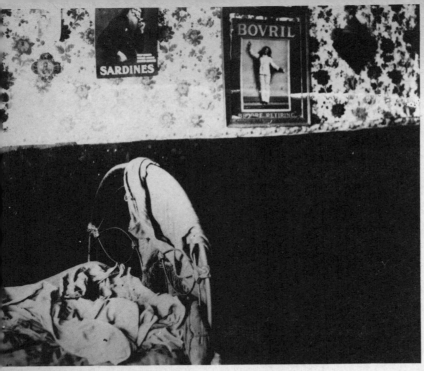

A tenement room, unfurnished, let at 7½p a week, Mercer Street, Dublin.

Furnished tenement in the Coombe, let at 17½p a week.

Tenement at 8 Waterford Street
(formerly Upper Tyrone Street).

about 1**s**. 6**d**. to 2**s**. I have got the exact figures for those two houses; I took them down this morning. The back parlour at No. 10 North Cumberland Street, is let at 3**s**.; the front parlour at 3**s**.; the front drawing room at 3**s**. 6**d**., the back drawing room at 3**s**.; what they call the two pair back in Dublin, that is to say the second storey is let at 3**s**.; the back of that at 2**s**.; and the whole of the top at 4**s**. That is 21**s**. 6**d**. altogether.

23,251. (**The Bishop of Bedford**.) Do any of the tenants occupy more than one room? — Yes, at the top sometimes, if they have a large family and can afford it. I also ascertained this morning some of their wages. One person paying 1**s**. 9**d**. rent has 20**s**. per week, and another paying 3**s**. rent has 16**s**. per week.

23,252. (**Chairman**) A rent of 1**s**. 9**d**. on a wage of 20**s**. per week is a very small amount of house rent? — Very small.

23,253. Was that a case of a family? — Yes, there were two or three children there. The man was a porter. Then there is one man paying 3**s**. 6**d**. who has 18**s**. per week, one paying 2**s**. 6**d**. has 20**s**. per week, and one paying 3**s**. has 30**s**. per week, but he is a printer, and he only gets work off and on. One house brought in 21**s**. per week and another 29**s**. per week. The house that brought in 21**s**. per week was the house that was bought for 105£., and the house was in excellent order from top to bottom and well cared for, and the people are very respectable. The other house occupied by people paying higher rents was not so well cared for, and they are not the same class of people.

The contrast between rich and poor lay in part in the mobility of the former. The poor had little choice, hence they congregated in cabins on cheap land or herded together more centrally in tenements in manufacturing or decaying residential districts. The growth of towns has always been characterised by the mobility of the well-off. In the eighteenth century, in Dublin the well-to-do abandoned the Liberties and the city for new districts to the north and to the east. The process was repeated in the nineteenth century with the well-off moving out to new suburbs and the poor invading the houses they vacated. As they left and districts degenerated into slums, property values fell.

Valuation of Houses in Henrietta Street

THOM'S DIRECTORY 1879		THOM'S DIRECTORY 1855		THOM'S DIRECTORY 1841	
	Valuation		Valuation		Valuation
No. 1, .	£13	No. 1, .	£20	No. 1, .	£25
„ 2, .	25	„ 2, .	35	„ 1½, .	32
„ 3, .	58	„ 3, .	100	„ 2, .	120
„ 4, .	55	„ 4, .	105	„ 3, .	130
„ 5, .	38	„ 5, .	75	„ 4, .	100
„ 6, .	30	„ 6, .	58	„ 5, .	80
„ 7, .	41	„ 7 .	76	„ 6, .	100
„ 8, .	39	„ 8, .	72	„ 7, .	100
„ 9, .	57	„ 9,	270	„ 8, .	150
„ 10, .	78	„ 10,		„ 9, .	170
King's Inns, .	500	King's Inns,	1,000	„ 10, .	80
No. 11, .	50	No. 11, .	66	King's Inns,	550
		„ 12, .	60	No. 11, .	100
„ 13, .	51	„ 13, .	88	„ 12, .	120
		„ 14, .	95	„ 13, .	120
		„ 15, .	52	„ 14, .	80
		„ 16, .	37	„ 15, .	60
„ 17, .	7	„ 17, .	28	„ 16, .	40
		„ 18, .	18	„ 17, .	—
		„ 19, .	20	„ 18, .	—
		„ 20, .	7	„ 19,	£31 10s.
	£1,042		£2,282		£2,288 10s.

The number of Dublin tenements, for instance, increased alarmingly in the second half of the nineteenth century; from 8,796 a decade or two previously to 9,760 in 1880. About 117,000 people lived in them at the latter date, though some 2,300 houses were considered totally unfit for habitation.

Tenement houses in most Irish towns had been built originally for the requirements of a single prosperous family and its servants. They had not been designed to accommodate several families, let alone a family to every room. Tenement houses were at their peak at this stage.

Slum houses were not characteristic of all towns. In the towns of the north-east, well-paid artisans were more numerous and even labourers' wages were supplemented by women's earnings in the

36

Early industrial housing, erected in the
1830s, in Sandy Row, Belfast.

Clearances at Linen Hall and Lisburn
Streets, 1913.

mills. In consequence, families here were able to pay higher rents on average than at southern wage levels, and the prospect of letting modest dwellings at an economic rent was sufficient to attract speculative builders into building working-class houses extensively. Since the 1870s local authorities had extended powers to supervise tenements, and the first clearances were undertaken in some of the worst slums in the Liberties. Decaying houses of the late seventeenth century were cleared away, a process which accelerated in subsequent decades. Many of these houses had no backyards at all. At the same time, under the auspices of philanthropists, artisan dwelling companies, and finally the local authorities, the provision of relatively cheap housing accommodation got under way. In Dublin between 1880 and 1914, the number of tenement houses was reduced from 9,760 to 5,322, their inhabitants from 117,000 to 87,305. Within the same period 6,656 artisan dwelling houses had been constructed to house some 32,000 people. The first steps, inadequate but nevertheless substantial, in urban rehousing for the less well-off had been taken. But though rents were low, they were not cheap enough for the poorest families. Relatively modest rents of 4/- or 5/- a house were still beyond the means of casual labourers and the very poor.

It would appear from the evidence given before us, and the statements submitted to us, that the following Companies and Societies have provided housing accommodation for the working classes in the city:

Extract from the report of the departmental committee to enquire into the housing conditions of the working classes in the city of Dublin (published 1914)

	Dwellings	Population	
Artisans' Dwellings Co.	3,081	13,938	
Iveagh Trust (not including Iveagh House)	586	2,026	
Iveagh House	1	450	(average)
Association for housing of Very Poor	157	810	
Industrial Tenements Co.	50	250	
City and Suburban Workmen's Dwellings Co.	288	1,645	
G. S. & W. Railway	149	870	(estimated)
Midland Great Western Railway	83	400	
A. Guinness & Co.	87	450	
Watkins & Co.	87	400	
Dublin United Tramways Co. ...	165	800	(estimated)
Messrs. Pile	90	500	
Mr. Patterson	36	180	
Vance's Buildings	180	780	
Earl of Meath	93	450	
	5,133	23,949	
Alexandra Guild	60	240	
Social Service Tenements Co. ...	77	272	
Corporation — (includes 8 labourers' cottages at Donnycarney)	1,385	7,500	
Lodging House, Benburb Street ...	1	100	
	6,656	32,061	Estimated

Eighteenth-century beggars

Barefooted woman and child in Dublin in the 1790s.

Living Conditions

Living conditions were grim for the ordinary people. There was some improvement in the nineteenth century, although it is difficult to assess it precisely. Beggars, though still they were many, were far less numerous in the towns than formerly. By the end of the nineteenth century while barefoot children were still to be seen, a barefoot adult, once a common sight, was now a rarity. Food shops were far more numerous, replacing the street stalls and door-to-door vendors of the eighteenth or early nineteenth centuries. Shops, with their higher overheads, suggest more regularity in purchases than other modes of distribution; credit by shopkeepers, while it created its own problems, helped to maintain purchases as well. A regular diet of tea, sugar and bread was beginning to replace older patterns of working-class diet. If more regular, it was however more monotonous than that of the eighteenth century when oysters, cockles and even artichokes, cheap and readily available at street corners, varied the erratic diet of the poor. Milk consumption however was low, to start with; and continued to remain so among the poor.

Alcohol played a large part in the life of the working-class. Disturbingly, observers thought that consumption of alcohol depended on the level of wages. Sobriety was induced by a fall in wages; an increase was spent on drink. This suggests demoralisation.

Barefooted children in Hacket's Court (Upper Kevin Street), 1913.

YOUG Sprouts, green Sprouts —
Fi: white Cabbage.—Here's the
white Cauliflower.—Come buye my ripe
Artichoke.

FINE Wall Cherries, ripe Wall Cherries.—A Penny a Quart, the ripe
Gooseberries, a Penny a Quart.

BUYE the large black Cockle, fine
large black Cockle;—Here's fresh
boil'd Crabs or Lobsters, here.

FRESH Herrings, large Dublin-bay
Herring, alive here.—Here's a large
fresh Cod alive, here.—Here's large Soles
or Places alive, or fine Buya Salmon.

Street vendors in eighteenth-century
Dublin cried out food items as varied as
sprouts, cabbages, cauliflowers,
artichokes, cockles, oysters, and cherries.

Many of the cattle which provided
Dublin's milk supply were housed within
the city. Stables and cow manure added
to the city's sanitary problems. The
detail shows two cows being driven
opposite the west front of St Patrick's
Cathedral.

Milk delivery in the eighteenth century
— Woman on horseback with milk can.

Street scene in the vicinity of Shandon, 1819.

The number of licensed public houses within the city is 582. The immorality and poverty of a large portion of the labouring poor, and particularly of the mechanics, are attributed by many to the constant habit of drinking whiskey; most of the witnesses consider that its use has increased. Two intelligent gentlemen, however, stated that it has rather decreased within a few years, and assign, as a cause, inability, on account of low wages to buy it.

Those who consider habits of drinking on the increase attribute it to the reduced price of whiskey, and to the facility of obtaining a licence of its sale.

The alteration in the law which has increased this facility by reducing the price of a licence to £2 on a house valued at £5, the lowest which is assessed, is generally represented as a great evil, and a wish is expressed that it should be raised to £10, or even £20, which would ensure a more respectable class of publicans, and diminish their number.

At the same time it is allowed that the facility given to the obtaining a licence has been a cause of preventing illicit sale, the licensed small vendors keeping a strict watch on their neighbours. Great advantage is represented to have resulted from not allowing the public houses to open before 7 a.m., and closing them at 11 p.m. Women with jugs evade, however, this regulation, and supply persons coming to market before that hour.

The consumption of beer by the lower classes has decreased. Such a regulation in the duties as would lower the price of beer, and encourage its use in preference to spirits, is considered very desirable.

A Temperance Society was established in 1831, and went on very well for a time; 100 to 120 persons became members: these,

Evidence of consumption of alcohol

A. In Cork city from the enquiry into the conditions of the poorer classes, 1836.

on obtaining a ticket from the secretary, more easily got employment. This led from 600 to 700 to join it, merely for that object; it then got into disrepute, and was given up.

Mr. **S. Lehan**, who has given attention to the subject of pawners, states that in 1800 there was only one pawn-shop in Cork; there are now 50. Several witnesses spoke of the evils resulting from them by the facility they afford to raise money on clothes, which is frequently spent on spirits. It was admitted, however, that they are often of great service, by enabling persons in distress to raise money on their goods, and thereby preventing starvation. Bishop **Murphy** considers that the introduction of establishments regulated as the Monts de Piété, in France, would be very beneficial.

Another example may be given of a house in Furze-lane, not so large as the above, in which there were 36 inmates, and only two ragged blankets amongst them; of the children three were quite naked, the others, and the women, covered with rags. The house and lane filthy in the extreme. This lane, indeed, was pointed out by Archdeacon **O'Keeffe** as about the most wretched in the city. These two instances, particularly the former, may be considered as a fair description of the majority of those who are described as destitute.

The streets of Cork are infested with importunate beggars, although constables are employed with orders to take them to the House of Industry; but in few cases is this done, the lower orders interfering to prevent the constables performing this part of their duty. Dr. **Bullen** states that a publican assured him that he had noted some of those beggars each to drink at his counter nine or ten glasses of whiskey in one day; the price of a glass is one penny or three halfpence, according to its quality.

Evidence of consumption of alcohol 3. In Dublin from the Evidence of Rev. Samuel Houghton, 13 October 1879, before Royal Sanitary Commission, 1879.

I think from my knowledge of the working classes in Dublin, that an increase in wages has led to an increase of actual poverty, because the people spend that increase not in comforts but on drink; and although they now receive a larger sum from their employers, they do not make as good use of it. I may mention, in order to show the condition of Dublin now with what it was twenty-five years ago, I have been twenty-five years Secretary to the Zoological Society of Ireland, and twenty-five years ago we considered that to admit the populace after divine service on Sundays at a penny per head was a good way of counter-acting the effects of the public houses. And some time ago, very much at the request of the working people themselves, when we found the gardens not in a satisfactory financial condition, we raised the admission to two pence, and there was no reaction. They find it now as easy to pay two pence as twenty-five years ago to spend one penny. The habits of the people have perhaps become a little lower than they were.

One of the striking features of the period was the deep demoralisation induced by crowded and unpleasant living conditions.

These conditions have existed for a century and a half; generation after generation were born under these, grew up under these; they were governed and controlled by them physically and mentally; the masses never conquered these conditions, nor rose above them; and the one fact borne in upon one is that they are largely impervious to their surroundings, and when pinched or hurt their trust in God for a better tomorrow is supreme. Nowhere did I find a revolt against the housing conditions: on the contrary, I found expressions of fear that anything was going to be done which would limit the tenements by the destruction of houses, and that they would be rendered houseless.

The worst feature of the housing conditions of the Dublin poor is the effect on children. In no city in these islands with which I am acquainted have the children such a freedom, I might say such possession of the streets, as Dublin. Many thousand little ones throng the thoroughfares, under no control, running moral and physical risks: ill-clad, ill-fed, ill-taught, undisciplined, how can they become useful citizens, or fathers and mothers of healthy children, serviceable to State and race? Numbers never rise out of slum life: they rush into matrimony at an early age, and the old process is repeated, 5 to 11 all told of a family in a single room, and the only change they can get is that to a neighbouring court or street, a rise or fall of a few degrees in their condition, or a short space in prison for drink or some petty offence. The woman left to herself in a single room with her children has no chance of cultivating any of the graces of life.

Donnybrook fair at a date before 1815. For the ordinary Dubliner the fair, held in August, was a major source of conviviality; for many their sole outing from the city in the course of the year.

Evidence of Mr. John Cooke, Hon. Treasurer of the National Society for the Prevention of Cruelty to Children, 24 November 1913, before the departmental committee to enquire into the housing conditions of the working classes in the city of Dublin.

44

She too quickly, as a rule, loses any she ever had. The little of a useful kind she was ever taught she forgets or has no chance of putting into practice. In all the rooms I saw no woman with a needle in her fingers, while there were plenty of tatters on her own and children's garments for the use of it and thread. Even were she inclined to cook, little could be done with the fireplace, while the shelf if not entirely bare, has seldom anything better than the materials for a poor tea. Under such conditions of living, under such uncertainty of means of a livelihood among large numbers, and with the drink habit so strong, it is very easy to account for the squalor and uncleanliness and general untidiness prevailing in the slum areas of the city.

The people in the tenement houses keep few pets — half a dozen dogs at the very most, and the same number of cats, sum up all I met of domestic animals; the notes of a bird in a cage never sound in the ears of those I visited, and not a flower in the window-sill brightens the tenement room. One copy of the **Red Magazine**, and that for firelight, was all the printed matter that met my eye in all the poor dwellings I entered.

In all the streets, alleys and courts I treaded there was but one spot where nature was called upon to produce something, and bountifully she responded. In a most forbidding corner I found a miniature chrysanthemum garden, due to a working couple in a poor court. There are many dark spots in the city that might be made bright if the example were followed.

Hours of labour were long; the search for alms or employment by the unemployed was itself time-consuming. Work-time and leisure were both spent within a limited and familiar area; outings further afield were rare, probably confined to one such as Dublin's Donnybrook fair, an annual event which attracted Dubliners in large numbers every August to its stalls and entertainments.

Water Supply

A water supply was essential for a town; pumps and wells could not cater for all its needs. Dublin had a supply from outside sources fed from the rivers Poddle and Dodder since 1275. Two watercourses carried the supply to the city and suburbs; one, the earl of Meath's water-course to the Liberties, the other, the city of Dublin water-course carried water to the basin at St James's Street, to supply the higher parts including the old city itself. This was still the main source of supply to the city in the eighteenth century. The problems were enormous; the water was increasingly dirty, wastage was extensive and unauthorised drawing from the open course rife. Nor was the supply available to all houses; in 1770 only 3,182 houses out of some 15,000 had a supply. In a populous street

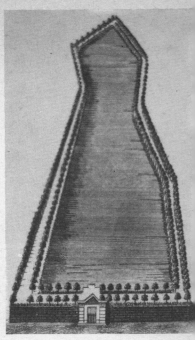

Dublin city basin, 1728, source of supply of the city water pipes.

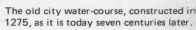

The old city water-course, constructed in 1275, as it is today seven centuries later.

7

Courfe from the Bason to the *Tongue*) I found the Channel for the moft Part choak'd with Weeds and great Seepage thro' the Banks, occafioned by their being irregularly difpos'd, and not made in the proper Manner; but what moft furpriz'd me, was, to find, in fome Places above *Dolphin*'s Barn, Breaches made in the Banks, and only ftop'd for the prefent with Sods, which ferve inftead of Sluices, in Summer, to let the Water run in fmall Channels through the adjacent Fields, for private Ufes.

As to the Wafte which happens after the Water is conducted into the Bason, that is occafion'd, 1ft, By letting the Water run in an open Trough behind *James*'s Gate. 2dly, By conducting the Water in Shores along *Thomas*, *Francis*-*Street*, and *Bridge-foot-Street*.

Now one great Difadvantage in fuffering the City Water to run in an open Trough is this, that the neareft Inhabitants to the Water-courfe will take the Liberty of ferving themfelves, and will draw

draw off what fhou'd have been diftributed proportionally, in fuch Quantity and Manner as they think convenient; without regarding the Injury done to the Publick. And this Obfervation is confirm'd by the real Practife of feveral People who live near the City-Water, fome of whom have a four Inch *Main*, others Cocks, leading from the Trough, which they open at Pleafure, and draw off the greateft Share of that Water which fhou'd fupply the whole City. Now this Damage is fo confiderable, that the 4 Inch *Pipe*, at a common Velocity, will deliver 75 Hogfheads *per* Hour, that is, near $\frac{1}{14}$ Part of the Quantity running through that Trough for the Supply of the whole City.

In making this Remark, I by no Means intend to deprive the Inhabitants of fo much Water as their Occafions may require, but only to prevent the too frequent Abufe. 2dly, The conveying Water through Shores is never practis'd where there is a Scarcity; for Shores can

can by no Means be made fo ftaunch as to hold Water without a confiderable Wafte. One quarter part is the common Allowance, which is a great Reduction of the City Supply.

A farther Inconvenience is, that thefe Shores cannot be funk deep in the Ground, People are apt to tear up the Cover when Water is fcarce, and fupply themfelves.

It is likewife, if (I may be allow'd to fay fo,) a Mifmanagement to have one of the three fix Inch *Mains* (which are fupply'd from the Bason) apply'd only for the Ufe of *James*'s Street, under Pretence that it is choak'd up. Therefore, to fet this, and the Manner in which the other Shores and *Mains* are carried in a clear Light, have fubjoined a Map of that Part of the City where they run, in which they are delineated, and to make the fame yet more intelligible, diftinguifhed by different Colours.

To conclude this *Confideration*, upon collecting together the feveral Abufes to which the City Water is liable, it appears

B   th

Dublin water-supply as described in Richard Castle's **An essay towards supplying the city of Dublin with water, 1735.**

The duty of the turn-cocks, 1771.

No. I.

THE DUTY OF THE TURN-COCKS.

EVERY Turn-Cock, in his refpective Ward, is to be careful to turn the Water to each Street, the Days and Hours fet down. He is to be diligent to find out Breaches or Stoppages in the Main Pipes, and to report the fame immediately in Writing at the Pipe-Water Office, that the Inhabitants that fuffer by fuch may be redreffed. When Breaches are in the Streets, or Houfes overflowed, he is, to the beft of his Judgment, to report, if he thinks it any Branch, that the City may not be put to any unneceffary Trouble and Expence. He is, in Time of Scarcity, to divide the Water among the Inhabitants as equal as he can, without Favour to any particular Street. He is to force all Branches that are ftopt in his Ward. He is to be obfervant and obedient to whatever Inftructions he fhall receive from the Overfeers of the Pipe-Water Works, relative to his Duty.

He is to attend where any Main Pipes are repairing or laying in his Ward, to turn the Water on and off, as Occafion fhall require. He is to attend where any Houfe is on Fire in his Ward, whether at Night or Day Time, and to turn all the Force he can of Water, where fuch Fire fhall happen; and when fuch Fire is extinguifhed, he is to turn the Water immediately to the proper Service. He is not

by any Means to leave the Keys of his Stop Cocks in any Huckfter's Cellar, or other Place where they may be taken away by Perfons for ill Purpofes. He is to carry a Crow and Scoope with him; the former for the Help of him to turn his Cocks, and the latter to take Gravel or Dirt from the Spends of them. He is to make Report in Writing every Day, at the Pipe-Water Office, of the Condition of his Ward, on Pain of forfeiting a Day's Wages for every Omiffion. He is not to demand Money, Drink, or any Gratuity from any Perfon, on account of relieving them in any of thefe Particulars, or for doing any Part of his Duty as a Turn-Cock. He is not to turn the Water from any Street, at the ufual Time of Service, at the Defire of any Plumber, or other Perfon, on repairing or affixing any Branch, on any Account, but for the Repairs of the Pipe-Water Works, or by the Directions of the Overfeers of faid Work. He is not to permit any Branch to be affixed on the Main Pipes, or bared or touched by any Perfon, unlefs faid Overfeers be firft acquainted, and give Directions for it. Or is any Turn-Cock to undertake to mend or affix any Branch, or to open or pave Ground, on any Account whatfoever.

Rutland Fountain, Merrion Square.

Women getting water from a fountain opposite St Catherine's Church, Thomas Street.

Water-cart to supplement the water supply, Belfast, c. 1870.

C H A P. XIV.

An Act for preventing the spreading of Fires, and for appointing of Watches in Cities and Towns-corporate.

Amended 13 & 14 G. 3. c. 24.

WHEREAS it is of great importance for the preservation of the lives and properties of the inhabitants of cities, that one fire-engine at the least should be provided and kept in every parish therein, and that regular watches should be appointed to prevent disturbances in the night: be it enacted by the King's most excellent Majesty by and with the advice and consent of the lords spiritual and temporal and commons in this present Parliament assembled, and by the authority of the same, that the minister of every parish in every city and town-corporate, except such for which particular provisions have been already made by some law,) or his curate, shall on the first day of June one thousand seven hundred and seventy two hold a vestry, of which he shall give publick notice at least six days previous to the holding of such vestry, including the day of such notice; and such vestry shall at such meeting determine and ascertain the sum of money to be raised upon the parish for the purpose of purchasing one fire engine at the least with pipes, buckets, and all other implements necessary for working the same, and for providing a proper place for keeping the same in, and shall appoint such persons to attend and work the same, as often as occasion shall require, at such yearly salaries as they shall think proper; and such vestry shall at such meeting elect and nominate three of the parishioners of good substance to be directors of the watch for the year ensuing, and shall also appoint such number of watchmen and at such wages, as they shall think proper, which watchmen shall be under the controul and inspection of such directors.

In every city or corporate town ministers or curates 1 June 1772 to hold a vestry on 6 days notice,

to fix a parish rate for 1 engine at least with all implements, and for keeping, and attendants, at yearly salaries,

elect 3 substantial watch-directors for the year,

and watchmen at wages under their controul.

II. Provided always, That no such parish, which has at present a fire-engine belonging to it, shall be obliged to purchase another.

III. And be it enacted by the authority aforesaid, That the minister of every parish or his curate, shall on every first day of June annually during the continuance of this act hold a vestry, of which such notice shall be given as aforesaid, for the purpose of chusing and appointing such persons directors and watchmen, as herein before mentioned, for the year ensuing; and such vestry shall at such meetings determine and settle what sums shall be

The like every 1 June.

like Plunket Street in one of the oldest parts of Dublin, even as late as 1860, only one of 700 houses had a piped supply.

Many relied on pumps or public fountains. In 1860 in the parish of St Paul's, Arran Quay, people went up to a half mile to get water; in St Laurence's parish, North Strand, 3,000 people relied on a single public fountain. Many purchased water at the inns. An expensive and inadequate supply was little used or worse re-used. The restricted supply itself was inadequate, and had to be supplemented from the Grand and Royal Canals for the south and north sides of the city respectively. The water was dirty, a carrier of disease; and springs and wells which supplemented the supply were themselves polluted.

A small supply meant a low pressure. Water would reach the top storey of the house only if a householder installed a pump to force it to that level. Low pressure meant that fire fighting was a virtual impossibility. Fear of fire had always haunted townsmen; thatched roofs had been a fruitful source of conflagration in medieval times although municipal regulation had, as a result of much effort, ousted most of the thatched houses from the walled towns. Conflagration remained common in the cabin districts, and fear of fire was little less universal in other districts. An act of parliament in 1772 required every parish to maintain a fire watch and service. But low pressures made fire services unavailing. One of the turncock's duties in the eighteenth century was to turn off water to other areas to raise pressure near the fire. Even as late as 1860, it took twenty minutes after the arrival of an engine on the scene before fire fighting could begin. But a sense of general responsibility for fire fighting was dimly awakening, and responsibility was no longer left solely to the parishes or to the insurance companies (who ran a fire service exclusively for the benefit of their customers): in 1860 the police in Dublin had a station for an engine and six hoses in Winetavern Street. Dublin's water problems were solved only with the introduction of the Vartry supply in 1867. About this time too, improved supplies were provided in other towns.

NINE o'Clock! Nine o'Clock! past Nine o'Clock, and a dark cloudy Night.

Dublin city-watchman. The watchman's role was of major importance when the fire threat was constant and fire service poor.

Newspaper reports of conflagrations: Limerick and Birr, 1778; Dublin 1787.

sent relief.

DUBLIN, *May* 14, 1787.
At five o'clock this evening a most dreadful fire broke out in the warehouse of Mr. Wall, grocer, of Patrick-street, which entirely consumed the same; but the timely assistance of different fire-engines, and the speedy arrival of Mr. Sheriff Fleming and the guard, the dwelling-house and neighbourhood were preserved, though the houses in Hanover lane took fire several times, and were as often extinguished.
This day his Grace the Lord Lieutenant went to the House of Peers, and gave the royal assent to the following bills.
The bill for the better regulation and collec-

Limerick, August 27.
LAST night a number of houses were consumed at Kilmallock, said to contain sixty families, and Mr. Fleming, a shop-keeper of a fair character, was unfortunately killed in attempting to escape through the flames.
. . . . generally thought will be hanged.
Birr, Aug. 31. On Friday night a most dreadful fire broke out in Mill-lane in this town, and being all thatched houses, 9 of them were destroyed before the flames could be extinguished. The inhabitants were chiefly poor industrious people, who had not time to save any thing of their effects worth mentioning; by which means they are almost reduced to a state of beggary; and had not the night been providentially very calm, in all probability great part of the town would have been consumed.

Early Dublin fireman, 1834.

Firefighting in Dublin in late eighteenth century.

Horse-drawn fire engine, Belfast. This engine was superseded only in 1892.

Tunnelling through Callow Hill, in Wicklow, 1864/6, preparatory to laying pipes to bring the Vartry water to Dublin.

Laying pipes, perhaps near Newtownmountkennedy, for the Vartry supply 1864/6.

Sanitation

Sanitation was a major problem in every town. Such sewers as existed were intended to carry away flood water.

No refuse was collected. Not even a privy existed in many houses, including a large number of tenement houses, some had not even an outside yard. Soil was dumped directly in the streets. Even the main streets were cleared only once a fortnight or so. Rain swept much of the soil direct into the sewers.

52

vidence of John Purcell, a cleaning
ontractor before the Irish Commons
ommittee on the state of pavements in
e streets of Dublin, 3 April 1778.

John Purcell says he was contractor for No. 3, South Side, at £119 per annum; has a farm within a mile of Dublin; carries his dung to Quaker-Hill, about a quarter of a mile from the Upper End of Kevin's-Port; believes he cleaned College Street about a fortnight ago; cleans it once a fortnight; Dame Street requires cleaning twice in a week; sometimes cleans Parliament Street once in a week, sometimes once in a fortnight, it is an advantage to let the streets lie long without carrying off the dirt; the dirt would be stiffer, and sooner drawn; then one cart will draw as much as three; some contractors let the dirt lie heaped for days; he cannot; his is the most troublesome lot; keeps four two horse carts and two sweepers between him and John Smyth; generally makes six turns a day; gives his men directions to do so; the carts are their own; pays their sweepers 1s. 1d. per day; the sweepers do nothing else; the drivers always load; in wet weather two sweepers can keep four carts going; the sweepers go on before the carts to prepare for loading.

These were the primitive arrangements of the eighteenth century; and there was little improvement in the early decades of the nineteenth century. In New Ross, as late as 1885, three quarters of the labourers' houses were reputed to have no sanitary arrangements, and even some 'respectable' houses were similarly unprovided. In the city of Cork, in the 1880s, the Corporation provided dust bins and boxes at the corners of the streets, especially where the houses had no sanitary arrangements, and these were cleared every morning. In many towns private contractors collected stable manure and night-soil for sale to farmers. In the back streets of towns conditions had little changed even as late as the 1930s.

diary account (December 30, 1950) of
anitary conditions in alleys in Killarney
nd Killorglin circa 1930.

This put me in mind of Ball Alley Lane, Huggards Lane and Brasby Lane. Ball Alley Lane 28 holdings, Huggards 18, and Brasby's 28. Cobbled roads, open cobbled drains in centres, no lavatories, no water laid on only a fountain at end of lane. Pigs kept and human manure added to the pigs' muck heap. I speak of years around 1930. All this manure had to be wheelbarrowed through the kitchen and passage out the front door into the lane, when the manure was sold. The yard would be about 20-10 feet.

The only sanitary accommodation outside the manure heap was a bucket which was emptied into the middle of the lane after dark, by those who did not want to sell manure. The stench was awful then. Luckily Killarney has a wet climate and the open drains then were cleared.

In these lanes every family was or looked consumptive, and the families were big. Fevers were frequent and diptheria [sic], typhoid and sometimes typhus, but there was a hush-hush policy, as the names of these diseases might frighten visitors.

Regarding Killorglin, when I used to travel there 1920-1930, I used to call on a shoemaker called C. . . He lived on the steepest part of the hill, in the main street. He lived about half way up, on the left hand side, as one ascended the hill. His house was near opposite that street, that Crowley the draper had his shop in. C. . .'s house was about 12 feet wide. One entered direct into his kitchen living-room and workshop, it was about 14 feet deep. I do not remember if there was a room at the back of his, but I think there was. An open drain a foot wide and about the same depth ran through the kitchen and under the front door, where it must have gone into a covered drain. I had pity for this man and his family, and I wanted to wash myself when I left him. He had a happy face, and a philosophy which enabled him to endure. He used to say 'everything happens for the best'.

Sewers, where they existed, had been intended simply to carry rainwater, not the soil of a city. They were built of rubble and were porous, hence once soil was thrown or carried into them, they readily became a source of infection. From the middle of the nineteenth century more satisfactory sewers were built in the towns. By 1879, some 58 sewers discharged into the Liffey from Kingsbridge down to the outlet of the Dodder. Before 1867 the water-closet was little known in Dublin because of the scarcity and low pressure of water. After 1867 the number of water closets rose rapidly: from 7,124 in 1880 they doubled to 15,531 in 1882, and by the end of the century the privy had been virtually completely replaced by the water-closet in the city. But water-closets revealed the weaknesses of existing sewers dramatically. Water-borne soil percolated through defective connections and through porous main sewers; at first the water-closet seemed to aggravate rather than reduce sanitation problems. Even the new sewers built after 1850 and intended to carry water-borne soil, were characterised by faults; first, poor connections from the closets in private houses to the sewer meant that soil percolated through faulty rubble drains and formed cesspools under the gardens of houses; and second, the poor ventilation in the sewers, the consequence of which was that sewer gases backed up in the sewers into the higher regions of towns and then entered houses.

The evidence tendered at our enquiry and embodied in this our Report, abundantly proves and in some degree confirms these remarks of the City Engineer, namely, that it will be a mistake to charge the exceptionally high death-rate which has for so long a period afflicted Dublin, exclusively on defective main sewering. Whilst we are willing to give the fullest credit to the Municipal Corporation and to their engineer for the improvements carried out in the Dublin sewers since the year 1851, we know by experience that, considering the circumstances under which they have worked, the main sewers of Dublin

Extract from conclusions of the Royal Commission's report on sewerage and drainage of the city of Dublin, 1880.

cannot be in that perfect condition claimed for them, as they are necessarily a patch-work system — irregular in line, in gradient, and in cross-sectional dimensions — they are not complete in side entrance and man-hole arrangements, nor in ventilation and gulley apparatus, as the evidence shows that these works are reported to be in progress at this time. Having examined the sections of the improvements carried out in the old sewers we admit that credit is due both to the Corporation and to their engineer for what has been done, but in the nature of things the main sewers of Dublin cannot be accepted as a perfect system, such as would be designed and carried out now if the work had to be commenced without the fettering consideration of how best to arrange, improve, and bring into fairly working order a rude, irregular, and roughly-constructed number of street and road drains. Dublin is, however, only in a condition with respect to its main sewering similar to what London, Liverpool, and other large towns were before the old and defectively designed, and badly constructed street drains were improved to better fit them for modern uses — as main sewers. One prime defect in old systems of town draining has arisen from a want of foresight in the design, but it will probably be nearer to the truth to say that there was an absence of design, and under the conditions, as previously explained, necessarily so. The sewers of Dublin at present form a network of continuous flue communication, so that any gases generated in the lower portions and along the margins of the river can flow along the sewers and drains uninterruptedly to the higher levels, rendering the higher portions and the suburbs which ought to be the healthiest districts, exceptionally unhealthy. The remedy for some of these defects may be provided in the main intercepting scheme of sewerage when this system is carried out. The high level intercepting sewers will prevent the water-logging and flooding of the low levels by the upland sewage, and if these intercepting sewers are properly designed and constructed they will also prevent the upward flow of sewage gases from the lower to the higher parts of the city.

The main sewers having been constructed from time to time; and not on the best plan that modern engineering would now devise, the City Engineer calculates that a further sum of £30,000 may be required to complete the main sewers. The old sewers were not ventilated, and are not, by any means, sufficiently ventilated at present. To the existing sewers, we may add 10 miles more for new streets, and there will then be about 120 miles of main-sewers to ventilate; and, as there should be for safety, not fewer than 20 ventilators on each lineal mile of sewer, there should be in the whole some 2,400 main-sewer ventilators. Towards this number we have been informed there are 400, all of which have been recently put down, leaving 2,000 to be added. This is a most important question for the Corporation and the citizens of Dublin, as sewers which are unventilated are unsafe. At present some of the sewer-ventilators recently opened on the main streets have been complained about as having been most offensive, and also as having caused disease. The reason is that the sewers as a whole are not sufficiently ventilated in other districts. There should be on the 120 miles of sewers not fewer than five hundred side-entrances or manholes, one thousand well-arranged street gullies, and 2,400 main-sewer ventilators. At all steep-gradients the sewers should be ramped, a sewer mouth-flap covering the sewer end delivering sewage from above. This flap will prevent sewage gases flowing to the higher parts of the city as at present.

For the former problem, the solution was in part the implementation of stringent standards for connecting drains; for the latter, in part better sewer ventilation and the installation of flaps to prevent sewer gases forcing their way into homes or streets. But the solution to the latter problem required even more ambitious works. Poor ventilation was contributed to by the main sewer outlets being blocked by the rising tide, shutting back the sewage and adding to the accumulation of gas. In Dublin, for instance, the solution lay in the construction between 1896 and 1906 of giant intercepting sewers along both sides of the Liffey to take the sewage to a central pumping station where liquid would be pumped into the sea, and solids after settling at the bottom of precipitation tanks were dumped far out to sea.

Two closets for seventy people — house in Newmarket Street, Dublin; note the pump in yard: this was the sole source of water supply for all the inhabitants of the house.

Dublin main drainage scheme: outfall
works in course of construction, showing
channel with sludge culvert under.

Dublin main drainage scheme: general
view of outfall works and new harbour
with sludge vessel, **T.S.S. Shamrock.**

Lighting

Extensive urban lighting by oil lamps was first achieved in the eighteenth century. It was not very efficient, and it was only with gas lighting in the early nineteenth century that street lighting became satisfactory. In the smaller towns gas lighting was only introduced in the 1850s or even later. The generation of electricity in the 1880s was the introduction of a new element, which seemed important but not revolutionary at the time. Some factories generated electricity to light the works; this supply was often extended to adjacent houses or to a village. Electric trams, beginning to replace horse-drawn buses in the 1890s, were another source of demand for electricity, and early tram companies generated their own supply. The first electrical light to flicker in Ireland was from a lamp outside the **Freeman's Journal** in 1880, and in the same year the Dublin Electrical Light Company was floated,

57

Henry Weſtray and John Ruſſell.

Weſtray ſays they contract for twenty Pariſhes annually; he gets 1. 12s. for each Light from the Pariſhes that have Globes, and 1l. 1s. 6d. where Lamps only; the Difference is becauſe the Repair of a broken Globe coſts him more than a broken Lamp. Lamps are not within twenty-two Yards tranſverſely, as ordered by Law. The Oil uſed in London is foul Spermaceti Oil; here it is Sun-fiſh and Rape Oil. Sun-fiſh is a hot quick Oil, Rape is a ſteady Oil, and both ſhould be mixed; Spermaceti is beſt, perhaps; 4s. a Gallon; he mixes one-ſixth of Sun-fiſh, or thereabout, with Rape, as it requires; he has two Ciſterns, holding 2200 Gallons each; puts about 300 Gallons of Sun-fiſh in each; Sun-fiſh Oil makes a Smoke; it is made in Galway moſtly, and its Price, of a hot Summer, when there is a good Take, is from 1s. 9d. to 2s. 4d. per Gallon; Rape Oil is from 1s. 9d. to 2s. 6d.

They give to their Lamp-lighters much more Oil than is uſed; their Men combine and inſiſt on more Oil than is neceſſary, and claim it before their Faces as a Perquiſite; their ten-hour Standard is ſeven Quarts and a Half, or ſixty Naggins for ſixty Lamps a Day. Their Men are obliged to attend at the Watch-Houſes all Night, and if a Penalty be inflicted for Neglect, they cannot recover againſt their Men; the Men had formerly 6s. 6d. now they have 8s. 8d. a Week for every ſixty Lamps. Weſtray ſays he has twenty-one Men, five whereof are employed in the Liberty. Ruſſell ſays he has eighteen Men, one whereof is employed in the Barracks, beſide Boys; they light all the Pariſhes between them but St. Thomas's, which has about 100 Lamps; St. Nicholas within about ſeventeen Lamps, and St. John's about ſixty-ſix. Spermaceti Oil ſmokes the leaſt of any; their Men ought to clean the Lamps once a Fortnight, but cannot be brought to do it; each of them has one good Man. They trim every Day by the Nail, and not by the Sciſſars. One Quarter of an Inch of Wick will laſt a Night; the whole Art lies in leaving out Wick enough; but this uſes more Oil. In London they have Pipe-burners; here they are Tongue-burners; eighty Lamps is too much for any one Man to mind. Some now light 130 or 140, from the Scarcity of Men; there are about four Men, and four only, out of employ in Dublin; Weſtray ſays there is 760l. due to him in the Earl of Meath's Liberty, they dreſs in London with Sciſſars, without taking out the Burners; they here take down the Burners, and dreſs them with their Nails; they light in a different Manner too; ſays it is very material to encourage the Sun Fiſhery; the whole Liver of a Sun-fiſh goes to Oil, and gives from ſeven to twelve Hogſheads, the Reſt is good for nothing. Whale Fiſhery is beſt for Oil; the Encouragement to Export of Rape Seed has encreaſed the Price of Rape Oil.

For the double Burners at the Mayoralty-Houſe and Poſt-Office he ſays double Price to his Men, and gives double Oil. Weſtray ſays he lights the two Liberties according to the Moon.

Evidence of Henry Westray and John Russell, contractors for lighting lamps, Dublin, 1778.

Dublin oil lamp, 1792.

Dublin oil gas station, 1824.

Lamp lighters attending to a lamp on Essex Bridge, 1790s.

Alliance Gas Company's works, Rogerson's Quay, 1843.

View of interior of Fleet Street electricity works, 1900.

which for several years supplied a small number of private consumers and also lighted some streets. The first municipal supply in Dublin came from a station in Fleet Street in 1892, which supplied a limited part of the central city; this source was replaced by a new station at the Pigeon House opened in 1903. In 1904 however, there were only 650 consumers, though by then electricity was used for street lighting.

One of the original steam turbine-alternator generating sets, Pigeon House generating station, Dublin, 1906.

Dublin Corporation electricity generating station, Pigeon House, opened 1903.

Transport

Medieval towns created few problems in transport: an inhabitant could walk from one wall to the other — a walk of a few hundred yards — in several minutes. But as towns grew, transport needs increased. The traveller who arrived in a packet boat at Ringsend required a coach to Dublin. Comfort and status demanded that the well-to-do did not soil their clothes in the dirty streets or rough it with the ordinary people. The sedan chair — carried by two bearers — was ideal for town conditions. Wider

60

Ringsend coach, 1680.

Sedan chair and hackney rank in College Green, 1753.

Sedan chair and hackney rank in College Green, 1753.

Dublin city horse buses in the 1850s.

streets were both cause and effect of the number of carriages. Carriages made walking in narrow streets even more disagreeable, and wider streets enhanced the hitherto doubtful utility of carriages within towns. The gradual move of the well-to-do out of towns in the nineteenth century increased traffic on the approach roads, especially traffic to agreeable areas such as Kingstown. The existence already of this source of traffic attracted the first railway in Ireland, opened in 1834; in turn the ease of travel by railway lured even more people to the suburbs.

om W. M. Thackeray's The Irish ketch-book, 1843.

Before that day, so memorable for joy and sorrow, for rapture at receiving its monarch and tearful grief at losing him, when George IV. came and left the maritime resort of the citizens of Dublin, it bore a less genteel name than that which it owns at present, and was called Dunleary. After the glorious event Dunleary distained to be Dunleary any longer, and became Kingstown henceforward and for ever. Numerous terraces and pleasure-houses have been built in the place — they stretch row after row along the banks of the sea, and rise one above another on the hill. The rents of these houses are said to be very high; the Dublin citizens crowd into them in summer; and a great source of pleasure and comfort must it be to them to have the fresh sea-breezes and prospects so near to the metropolis.

The better sort of houses are handsome and spacious; but the fashionable quarter is yet in an unfinished state; for enterprising architects are always beginning new roads, rows and terraces; nor are those already built by any means complete.

The capabilities of the country, however, are very very great, and in many instances have been taken advantage of; for you

he process of suburban growth: the llage of Dalkey from Killiney c. 1830; e same view today.

63

see, besides the misery, numerous handsome houses and parks along the road, having fine lawns and woods, and the sea in our view, at a quarter of an hour's ride from Dublin. It is the continual appearance of this sort of wealth which makes the poverty more striking, and thus between the two (for there is no vacant space of fields between Kingstown and Dublin), the car reaches the city. There is but little commerce on this road, which was also in extremely bad repair. It is neglected for the sake of its thriving neighbour, the railroad, on which a dozen pretty little stations accommodate the inhabitants of the various villages through which we pass.

By mid-century horse-drawn buses had appeared on several routes bringing citizens from comfortable new suburbs like Rathmines to the centre of the city. Horse-drawn trams replaced buses in the 1870s which in turn were superseded by electric trams at the end of the century.

A horse tram. Note how the driver tur the horses before arriving at the point No writers record seems to survive of this technical procedure.

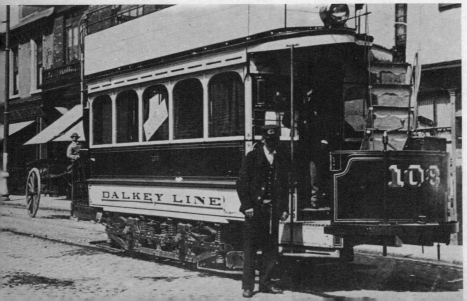

Early electrical tram about to leave Dalkey for Ballsbridge, c. 1898.

DALKEY LINE

109